"Quick, effective motivational & marketing
messages driving you to success"

"Use my time! Use my time! USE my time!!"

Vol. 13 In The *Sub 4 Minute Extra Mile* Series

by

Ted Ciuba

"Use my time! Use my time! USE my time!!"

Vol. 13 In The *Sub 4 Minute Extra Mile* Series

ISBN: 978-1478371847

by **Ted Ciuba**

www.HoloMagic.com
info@holomagic.com
Parthenon Marketing Inc
2400 Crestmoor Rd #36
Nashville TN 37215   USA

Orders & Enrollments
+1-877- *4 RICHES*
***
phone +1-615-662-3169
fax: +1-615-369-9749

 Contact Ted Ciuba about speaking for or training your group or organization.

Ted Ciuba is also the author of the incredible modernization and empowerment of Napoleon Hill's success classic, *Think & Grow Rich!*

Ted Ciuba
The New Think & Grow Rich
Author of Sub 4 Minute Extra Mile Series
Author of *The New Think And Grow Rich*

Tamara Doris

T.J. Rohleder

"This is **more than just a revamp with modern examples** - it radically transforms the vision by adding new gender, cross-cultural and international issues to the mix, including new material to include both science and genetics, as in the Quantum reality of accelerating income and wealth.

An excellent re-do of a classic financial inspirational guide."

"The writing is so much more applicable and understandable that I am literally forcing my friends, colleagues, and mastermind members to get their copies now!

Every page fills me with passion and revs me up!"

"I picked up Ted's book -- AND I WAS SHOCKED AND AMAZED! I sat there and began going through it ... and all of a sudden looked up and over 3 hours had gone by!!! I quickly read it from cover to cover within 2 days and then turned around and did it again! Ted has done a truly amazing thing, by totally re-writing this powerful classic. Every entrepreneur and business owner simply MUST have Ted's book!"

TABLE OF CONTENTS

CONTENTS

Vol. 13 In *The Sub 4 Minute Extra Mile* Series

"USE MY TIME! USE MY TIME! USE MY TIME!!"

by

Ted Ciuba

Introduction: It Takes So Little To Excel

As an achiever, would you agree with me that you must go the extra mile? *I thought so...*

Surely you know if you do what average people do, you'll get the same kind of average results they do. And something tells me you're a cut above that!

And it's actually quite easy to stand out, because most people wouldn't dream of going the extra mile. But for you and me, while, yes, it takes something extra, yes, it takes drive and discipline.... The amazing thing is, it takes so *little* to excel!

Roger Bannister
Runs Sub 4 Minute Mile

After all, it's called the extra *mile*, not the extra *100 miles!*

Be that as it may, we're talking about the positive rewards that come to you in any economy by going the extra mile.

It was Roger Bannister who defied and redefined history by running the sub 4 minute mile.

And the amazing thing is that Bannister did NOT spend the countless hours and hours practicing that conventional training would guide him to. He gave it what he could... In his busy pre-med Oxford schedule he took a mere 30 minutes out of his daily lunch hour to train and run. And with that he set a world record that had towered 3,000 years!

He ushered in a new era of possibility. Though no one had *ever* broken it, within 2 1/2 years time of Bannister's record-breaking, seemingly unachievable sub 4 minute mile, 18 others were doing it.

And how did he do it?... It wasn't a function of *time*. Conventional sports training encompasses hours on an almost daily basis, not 30 minutes!!

It was *intention*. Roger Bannister, in the short, focused, regular, intense, intended few minutes per day he wrested from his busy Oxford pre-med studies was throwing himself into the sport. He gave it everything he could, as an additional interest and pursuit in his life...

You see, when Roger Bannister suffered the ignominious defeat of coming in 5th place in the 1952 Olympics, right then and there, he determined to be the first human to run the sub 4 minute mile!

It was just a "thought". It's just another instance and undisputable illustration, my friend, of the power of intention powered by determination.

Moments before 6 pm on 6 May 1954, he takes a breath of vision and determination. He feels it! He confides to his pacemakers "The sub 4 minute attempt is on!"

Short moments later the shot is fired... The runners are off!! Roger Bannister breaks the string at the end of the mile in 3 minutes, 59 seconds, and 4/10's, trailblazing into the sub 4 minute mile age!

Recognition Point!! - This was NOT an unintended event! Recognition point!! Little efforts, little accomplishments - short, focused, regular, intense, intended training sessions - gear into colossal events!

Also note how little it takes to stand waaay beyond the competition! Roger Bannister redefined history in one evening... And he did it only with the razor's edge of difference, 1/10 of a second over 1/2 of a second!!!

This didn't happen by circumstance... Roger Bannister didn't "drift" over the finish line into the annals of history... It was the thing he geared all his intentions to accomplish, even though he didn't spend hours and hours a day in the quest to achieve it.

Which gives rise to the name of this series, The *Sub 4 Minute Extra Mile* Series...

Now you, honoring Roger Bannister's history-setting accomplishments and methods, can make the same kind of history-breaking progress in sub 4 minutes a day! Defy the status quo in short, focused, regular, intense, intended training sessions and redefine what's possible and what you accomplish!

HOW MUCH MONEY CAN IT MAKE?

People who become outrageously successful have a totally different outlook on outlays. Of course, they're not employees. No, they don't ask, "How much does it cost?" If they did, they'd always get the cheapest car, the cheapest advertising, the cheapest printing job, the cheapest, most affordable employee. Wouldn't they?

No, the correct way to phrase the question is, "How much can it *make*?"

Look, if you want an advertising scam that doesn't work, send me $2,000 and I'll post you to 2,000 websites. Honest to goodness, I really will. But they're so overused, overworked, they're places that nobody goes to, so it wouldn't do you *any* good.

On the other hand, if you want an ad that works, give me $9,000. I'll get a graphic designer, I'll get a copywriter, and I'll put you into a good magazine—and you'll be flooded with leads. You'll have the *real* opportunity to make money. Your investment will pay back 40-fold, 70-fold, 100-fold.

You see, it's not, "How much does it cost?" It's, "What is the wisdom?" It's, "How much money can it *make*?"

NOTES

Item / passage / page	Insight	Action

IT'S NOT HOW MUCH SOMETHING COSTS

The very first conference that I attended as an entrepreneur (I had attended a number of others in academia and in my corporate marketing career) cost me what I thought was an outrageous sum at the time— $1,100!

And then I attended another one shortly thereafter that offered resell rights to certain products, and it cost $3,000! And *then* I had a man offer to teach me how to do speaking and promoting, and those two events cost $20,000! Can you see the progression?

Now, granted, I don't want to downplay the fact that I was already in motion when I invested $20,000. I was somewhat in motion when I invested $3,000, but I was coming from a dead stop when I invested $1,100. Of course that was years ago…what that would be for you today you'd have to find out. You'd have to make your own mark.

But I'm telling you, *that* investment, combined with *my* effort, has yielded millions of dollars.

There's a tremendous yield in education, but that's not the main point at task here. It's…

It's *not* how much something costs, but how much something can *make* you that is your touchstone for evaluating if it's a good investment or not.

NOTES

Item / passage / page	Insight	Action

IT'S JUST COMMON GOOD SENSE

Surely you've heard of the 80/20 rule. Basically it says that we spend 80% of our time, efforts, energy, and resources doing the things or working with the clients that only give us 20% of our results. In other words, we waste a lot of time.

There's another way to use that 80/20 rule, and that's to take your quality time and make sure you're investing it on your high-priority tasks, the things that you've decided are the most important. For instance, making phone calls to ongoing prospects, instead of reading a book, which you know you must read, *might* be appropriate, during the prime business hours. Getting out and rubbing bellies.

Always remember, there are *prime* business hours – everything else is ancillary. Use the prime business hours for the things that most directly bring the revenue in.

You do have to do *both,* of course, but you know the difference between time-wasting activities and results-producing activities. It's about time and resource management.

And that brings up another thing. In the direct response marketing field, we do what we call sending out lead generators. We run an ad and we try to get people to raise their hand, so to speak, to identify themselves as being interested in what we have to offer. And then we begin to invest money, time, energy, and resources to follow up with them.

We do NOT simply buy a list, and send everyone out a dazzling expensive direct mail package.

Now, in the business world, that's just common good sense. That's the way thoughtful, conscious businesses do it. We broadcast to the many; we work with the select few. We send out the low-cost lead generator to the entire list, and those who respond (numerically sometimes very small in comparison to the "universe" we sent to), THOSE are the ones we send the expensive dazzling package to. They've told us they are interested, right now, in what we have to offer.

And I specifically think the same way about the clients and people that I work with.

Again, I'm in the direct response business, the information marketing business, so I'm putting a message out. And one of the ways I do that, of course, is that I've got my lead generator book, which is a really good kind of lead generator. A lead generator is a low cost, low involvement interest indicator. It's something a person proves through their purchase they have an interest in. You give first.

And the way the law works, you get. Importantly… You now know you're dealing with an *interested party*, and you now sick your marketing machine on them.

The people who respond are the ones we work with. Well, what do we have to give? Let's look at this. On the "human potential" side of the fence, we have education, we have motivation, we have empowerment. But every single one of those things has to be consumed and assimilated by the other party.

On the "marketing" side of the fence, we bring increased revenues, multiplied profits, and more time off to enjoy your good fortune.

Profits, you can see. Let's talk about human potential.

You can't count or touch education, motivation, or empowerment. Now, notice that I didn't say books, audios; and videos, because those are the forms we deliver education, motivation, and empowerment in. But for people to get the benefit, they have to *do* something with it. Can't "touch" it - though you can see and measure it!

And that's why we're not trying to just dump books on every corner, like you would with the Yellow Pages. That's why we only want to work with those who want to work with us.

Because it takes a lot of our sincere interest, *sincere* investigation, love, respect, admiration, desire, and, yes, money, for our clients to see a light, for them to improve—for them to make quantum improvement, that millimeter of improvement that can have a quantum effect wherever they're at.

Remember, we're in our 20% area now. We are with them, and it requires a lot on our part. We spend 80% of our time working with clients who want what we have to offer. That's another good reason to follow the 80/20 rule.

If we were involved with and getting beat up by the 80% of people who *didn't* want our message, *wouldn't* follow through, and we were on a *savior* campaign—well, life would be a lot different and difficult. And we sure wouldn't make as much money.

Get productive, resourceful, and profitable - put the 80/20 rule to work the right way in *your* life. Analyze it. Make it happen!

NOTES

Item / passage / page	Insight	Action

BEYOND THE MEASURE OF DOLLARS AND CENTS

One of the greatest things about being involved in and around a motivational and sales training business is the actualization that comes, in addition to our prime target. For instance, when I go into an enterprise, my target may be to increase productivity, to increase sales. That's what we're normally focused on - not in operations but in marketing.

And I'll tell you, there are so many different nuances, so many different manners of thinking that you need to get into the subconscious mind—and so it's a real jazz doing it. But one of the results of increasing sales is a better manner of life altogether, top to bottom, through every dimension. We call it actualization.

When you're actualized, feeling at the top of your game, creative, nimble, eager, enthusiastic, full of exuberance as a result of the training and acting on the training, doing the analysis, the study, the practice and getting it going—well, just that feeling *alone* has a value that makes everything you do better.

Because "you're coming from such a better place."

The character and quality of your actions are more open, more concerned, more loving, more thoughtful, more in tune with your bigger plans. No, nothing develops by itself. And we always say, "Find everything perfect, even while you're working to change it. But *enjoy* the new life that you have created!"

Because *that* is a joy *also*, a joy beyond the measure of dollars and cents.

NOTES

Item / passage / page	Insight	Action

WIN-WIN-LOSE

For me, the way I play the game is not win-win and it's not win-win-win—it's definitely win-win-lose. That's what I *definitely* have in mind.

My definite and precise intention is that my customer, client, or prospect wins with my offer.
Because if I can't pull that off, #1, I don't deserve their trust and their business, and #2, I won't *receive* their trust and their business on a repeat basis. And the only long-term plan that works is to have repeat customers, so you don't have to beat yourself up reselling all the time.

You *must* be a value creator for your clients.

So of course my customer or client is going to win, and of course, it does matter and my friends, clients, and protégés can pick up on it that in my heart is the most genuine, sincere desire, that really drives me at all hours of the day and night to deliver the education, motivation, and empowerment that helps them achieve the things they've always wanted so they can *move* to the next level.

Of course, I win; I'm expecting money back from setting that up. And my customers and clients know that. It's win-win. The *value* of what I deliver makes the dollars, Euros, yen, or whatever they give me worth the price.

So what is this about *win-win-lose*? Well, it's real simple—that "lose" is my competitor. Yes, we are in an enlightened age, and I do love and respect every single one of my competitors. Essentially, they are people with normal human desires and struggles just exactly like you and me, and for this, they deserve to be loved, respected, and honored.

I encourage you to do the same thing. I would never perform any overt act against them in any unethical or immoral way—no way.

On the other hand, I'm *certainly* working to get the money that my client list, my prospect list, has to spend on self-development and achieving and exceeding their goals in business and in life – income and otherwise. And I'm certainly looking to get a larger share of it than my competitors get, taking it away from them if that's where my potential customers are spending it currently.

The truth is, and I don't mean to be self-serving... Many, if not most, of my competitors are more interested in the money they can get from their customers than they are in their customers... Most of them aren't making any money on the plan they're promoting, but are making their money *selling* the plan they're promoting. So it's no mis-characterization to imply they are inept, greedy people who don't have your best interests at heart...

So, when we're talking competitors, I'm there to out-perform them, to out-deliver them, and to win grateful, loyal, repeat customers from them.

That's the nature of *business*. That's the nature of sports. Think football—win-win-lose. The team's out there, you're on the team, you're wanting your team to win. Obviously, you're thinking of the fans and delivering for them, because that's going to help you and you're going to have more fame, more money, more momentum as a result. *There's your win-win.*

But it's deliver first.

So you want to deliver to your fans—your clients/customers. You want to deliver for yourself and your team—you're going to get something out of it, too. And to deliver the optimum result for your fans and for your team – including yourself, naturally – you marshal all your training, experience, and efforts to beat the opposing team. *There's your lose.*

It's a zero-sum game: somebody wins, somebody loses.

Win-win-lose. Think it over. Maybe you've been too friendly; maybe you've been too open. Maybe some of your competitors have been laughing at you behind your back. Maybe it's time for you to get *serious* about winning the game, and not just having a few nice encounters.

IT HAS TO BE THEIR DECISION

I spend the vast majority of my time trying to guide and help people and entrepreneurs, and even let them know they need to *wake up.* **Wake up!** Now, those are the ones I'm dealing with as clients - to dress up their character, increase the income, multiply their profits, reduce their stress, and increase their contribution and their joy.

But even then, I have to sell them—even then, even while I'm waking them up. People ask, "Why do you use NLP?" It's because I'm using it to persuade people. And if I must use subconscious programming to help people move up the ladder to their highest and best self, I must. It's what God has given me to do.

And I teach these same principles to business people, to salespeople.

Psychologists tell us that most of our actions are unconscious—they come from the subconscious. We don't know why we do them… they're unexamined. Most people have no real rhyme or reason about knowing why they buy, for example.

Of course, we who study marketing know why they buy. We know it's for emotional reasons. We know they're hurting, they have poor self-esteem, they want more. They want more health, they want more looks, they want more body, they want more esteem, and, of course, they want more money, they want more time, and they want less stress. We know that.

And, since we've learned what they want, it's up to us to deploy different *triggers* to get them to buy.

Important Note: There's a book titled *Triggers: 30 Sales Tools You Can Use To Control The Mind Of Your Prospect To Motivate, Influence, and Persuade* by Joe Sugarman, and another by Robert Cialdini called *Influence: The Psychology Of Persuasion,* and my own book, co-written with Nathan Blaszak, *Subconscious Selling,* that deal with these themes. I highly recommend them all.

The idea is, we can incorporate in our presentations and demonstrations things prospects will respond to that may be below the radar for them. They may not know they're responding for unconscious/emotional reasons, but it will appeal to them.

Cialdini calls it the "click-whirr" response. (Like Pavlov's dogs – ring bell, dogs salivate.)

Such as asking small involvement/promise questions at the beginning of a presentation, and then moving into deeper territory. People want to be consistent. Like upselling after the initial sale is closed.

Such as letting them know that you truly like, admire, and respect them. (You can't fake this.) Such as letting them understand—because everybody likes to feel this—that they're secretly better than you. That disarms them.

Such as letting them in on the obvious truth they already know, that, frankly, most vendors just don't get it, and don't measure up.

Such as letting them know that *everybody* else is doing this, because they want to be like everybody else. They want to be in the in crowd.

This is not the place to offer a study on these items, as much as it is to say that when you understand the important aspects of persuasion, you can set up your presentations so that you incorporate the things which will trigger them into the buying response. And they'll never even know why. They'll just feel good about their choice.

Because it has to be their decision.

THINK CONSCIOUSLY AND GROW RICH

There's a kind of thinking that you need to understand, so that you can use it in the times that may be most important—like right now, in these tough economic times.

If someone is to lose their main source of income, it can put them in a tough situation immediately. That is the truth. Those are the facts. But there's a kind of thinking…we talk about "think and grow rich." The real truth of it is, we're talking about thinking consciously—or, "Consciously think, and you will grow rich."

Because you're thinking, and you're growing whatever it is that you're thinking anyway—so we're talking about getting conscious on it.

But here's the whole point. So you lose your job, and suddenly you go into panic mode: "What am I gonna do? How am I gonna feed my family? I'm gonna lose the house, I'm a failure!"

The fact of the matter is, it might be a good time to take stock. Take inventory. Think of the future as you *want* it. Maybe you were in a complacent place anyway. Think of the future as you want it, and now go about doing what you can to create it. Take stock. What kind of skill sets do you have? What extra time do you have that you could use? Who needs what you can offer? Where can you expand that you've never thought of before?

What other type of promotion, or product, or industry, can you go to work for and do?

You see, even though there are a lot of people looking for work, the creative people are always busy. Good people are still hard to find, and still in demand. Become good at it; do it.

See, if you think and nurture the panic thoughts and the fear thoughts, these issues become more *monumental* in your eyes, and they mount up and become as *giants* before you.

Sure, a sudden change can trigger a hyper state. But it's how you interpret the arousal, how you direct it that makes all the difference in the world.

Instead, think of them with your end in mind, in confidence, moving forward with a plan in action, not without adventures, with a vision. You're motivated and animated all over again, and everything you do has a different character. Every act takes you a different place.

You're not in the middle of the ocean, paddling like crazy, wearing yourself *out* trying, just being fearful. You're in the ocean, rhythmically breathing, paddling towards your goal. In other words, simply what you think makes all the difference in the world in what you accomplish and what you don't.

What you *think* is the seed for the experience you are moving on in your life.

KNOWING THAT IT'S YOURS

One of the concepts that people have challenges with, sometimes, is the state where we talk about knowing that something is yours, and not focusing on the lack. While you still physically don't have what it is you want—*physically* is the key word here—you should still affirm, desire, and *know* that it is yours. The position, the income, the freedom from debt, or whatever it is you want.

Let me try to explain that again. It's not a matter of being so blind that we don't realize that there is an *appearance* that you don't have what you desire. It's that you already are so connected with getting it, manifesting it, developing it, that there is no doubt in your mind that you *will* have it, you *will* find a way, you *will* do whatever it takes to manifest the thing. And, in fact, though it's not physically present at the moment, it *is* in the process of manifestation.

It's a mindset; it's a change of point of view. Instead of *"Woe is me, pobre John, Poor ol' John,"* you look towards the experience of what you want and you develop the feeling that it's already yours. You *will* get it. It's not a false bravado—it's an excitement, filled with belief, that comes from every fiber of your being that you're, *pow*, on the *path*!

You are presently *making* it, *manifesting it*! You *will have it*, just because you are doing what it takes. It just hasn't arrived yet, but it is yours…

And that's not to say you won't do experimentation, we always know that. You are doing what it takes. You have the factual knowledge that you're ultimately going to arrive at your destination. *That* gives you joy today. *That* gives you passion today. *That* lets you look past some of the "problems" that might be in your environment *today*.

So *decide* what it is you want in whatever situation you're in, and give it *every ounce of passion and belief, knowing* it's going to materialize because you do what you need to *do*! *That* is the kind of attitude, the kind of belief, natural order—the order of seed first, plant, then fruit.

An acorn in the ground never doubts it will live it's life as a tall, sturdy oak tree… And it gives it everything it's got to make it so!!

It's natural order you use to manifest the desires and dreams of your heart.

WHEN THE NEW WAYS ARE NOT YET KNOWN

My mother-in-law recently lost her husband of over 53 years. Another friend of mine recently suffered a divorce, and lost a child and economic stability in that event. A third lost her perfectly healthy, achieving husband on a single morning, without warning. Heart attack.

A number of us are involved, right now, in a turbulent economy. An economy that is taking a lot of victims, a lot of people hostage—a lot of people who aren't resourceful and don't know what to do about it, and think about the problems rather than what solutions they could deploy. A lot of people are hurting, while a lot of other people are getting by just fine.

But here's the whole thing—whether it's from death, divorce, or depression, there is always something, *always* somewhere, always happening to somebody that gives them a big knock on the head. That, *wow,* knocks their feet right out from under them and gets them up, wondering, "*What* happened?"

"*What* am I going to do when the old ways are not the new ways, and the new ways are not yet known?"

It's a rite of passage. It's a time that comes with turbulence. And it's a skillset that you should be prepared for, since this does happen. You should adopt and adapt. You should know this for yourself, and also to guide others.

When the old ways of doing things no longer exist, for whatever reason, in whatever dimension, do what you know to do—stop, diagnose, plan, and take action. Not with fear, but with the knowledge that, with consciousness and design, you can create whatever you want.

Take stock. Take inventory of what you have, what assets, what you *want*—dream most of all about what you want. Make a plan—how are you going to get it? To retrench is not the big issue. These events happen to everybody in life. And there doesn't have to be an economic depression going on, by the way, for some individual to lose their job with no warning.

At least today, anybody who loses their job has plenty of warning. Their company may not have warned them, but the economy sure has.

The answer's always the same—individual responsibility. Follow the six-step Formula for Riches - it works on both a macro and a micro scale.

Here's the quick sprint version… For the full version, I refer you to chapter one of the book, *The New Think And Grow Rich.* You need to have instant recall and recitement of your definite chief aim, however you define it in these simple six steps…

1. How much?
2. By when?
3. How?
4. Plan it.
5. Affirmatize it.
6. Program it.

Go back, find out what you want, do all your resourceful planning, create what you can create, decide these goals, and when, where, how. Put something on paper, start making it happen, make affirmative affirmations. And enter into that magical, mystical state of *belief! Believe,* and you shall have it!

You always *act* in accordance with your beliefs.

One significant philosopher said, "Only believe, and the thing shall by yours." Believe—it's that connecting with the end in that spirit of belief. Of course, you have to know where you're going. It's *that* that brings the power of the universe to bear for you!

You see it again… *That*'s HoloMagic.

A DEFINITE INTENTION TO FULFILL YOUR DESIRES

In *The NEW Think and Grow Rich,* there's the story of Edwin Barnes. And even though we didn't write it, we *could* be talking about the story of someone that you may know, Alex Mandossian. The principle I've seen both of these individuals use to succeed is available to anyone.

So what is that principle? First of all, they're both sharp guys—they *can* follow through on what they intend to do. But *oooh,* that's the word. They have made *definite* decisions about what they *intend* to do. And *that's* what they're doing.

The fact is, they're enjoying *outrageous* success *now*—but they both began with nothing. *Nothing* but a definite desire. Nothing but a determination to make it work. Other than that, they had nothing that any other capable, normal, human individual isn't possessed of. Now, what made it work for both of them?

What made it work was that they had the definite intention to fulfill their *desires*, nothing else.

Both of them are very sharp, both of them are business people, both of them know about testing, both of them know about getting advice from mentors, and both of them keep their heads straight, obviously with the right kind of input. Nope, what they had was a definite chief aim and the determination to accomplish *that*.

Now, you *can* decide on a definite chief aim. How did Barnes know that *his* definite chief aim in life was to be the partner of the preeminent businessman/inventor Thomas Edison? I don't know. We lead people through a lot of HoloMagic exercises to help them find it for themselves, but Barnes hasn't told me.

And neither has Alex Mandossian, even though he's a personal friend and associate. He has spoken at some of my events, and we've spoken at other events together—but all I know, to be honest, is what I've seen. That *is* a form of evidence gathering.

And *that* in both cases has convinced me. They *chose* a definite chief aim. Alex Mandossian apparently chose information marketing, liberty, the Internet, working part time, and a good income. That's what he chose, and that's what he's received.

Here's what *I* know— time is passing. It would *behoove* you to decide right now. If you could only do one major chief thing in your life, in your years on Earth, what that would be?

Once you do that, all your forces, all the forces of the universe—and you are a representative of the universe—will coordinate, connect, interconnect, and interact to bring you directly to the things you visualize *with your heart*.

BURN YOUR SHIPS BEHIND YOU

When Hernán Cortés invaded the coasts of Mexico, even though he had the overwhelming advantage of armor and gunpowder and firearms, he had troops who really didn't want to face the *unknown*, the *savages*, the *multicolor* painted beasts! Oh no, Hernán did not have a troop of ready soldiers.

So he did something that you might find advisable in your moments of partial success. The man *had* arrived at the shores of Mexico, and the ships had arrived intact. They *were* equipped to fight. They *were* trained. Now it's showtime. And what he did was just put that old proverb into action. There was no other option—he burned his ships behind him.

In fact, the phrase "burn your ships behind you" comes from what Hernán Cortés actually *did*. He burned his ships to put an end to the rebellion, to the mutinous thoughts, to the *crybabies*! In other words, he let everybody know one thing—and this is something that can help you, too. I'm not writing about this for good looks!

He let them know that they were not going to leave that place easily. They were committed to fighting the fight and living on the land they were now invading.

They were committed. Most of us say things like, "I'm gonna start this job part time," or "I'm going to start this business part time, and I'm gonna see…" I'm not saying don't do that, but I'm saying that others just get a few wiggles and then *jump* into it!

Doing that leaves no way back. Edwin Barnes, Thomas Edison's partner—that was his secret. Hey, myself, Ted Ciuba, I left California and came to Tennessee without a job in 1994—and I've never worked for anyone else since. And it was, "*This is* the way it's going to be."

It works the same way for all of us… we're not different. By the way, in my case, on January 1st, 1994, I set myself a goal (a command, really) that I was going to be *out of* California and *in* Tennessee before the sun set on the year 1994. I made it on December 27, but it *was* before the year ended. Funny how HoloMagic works.

Burn your ships; leave yourself no method of retreat, and you *will* get resourceful. *That's* what Hernán Cortés called on in his moment of jeopardy, *achievement,* career—and fame that endures forever!

THE ACCUMULATION OF RICHES AND THE HUMAN LIFE CYCLE

Here's a moment of insight, while it's actually happening, in the life of an author. I am reading my Spanish translation of *The NEW Think and Grow Rich*. They call it *El Nuevo Piense y Hágase Rico*. And I come across this line, "*La acumulación de dinero no puede dejarlo al azar, a la buena fortuna, a la suerte.*"

Now, I'm not going to assume, since you're in a primarily English audience at this moment, that you fully understood that. Let me tell you exactly what it says in English:

"The accumulation of riches cannot be left to chance, to good fortune, and to luck."

Chance, good fortune, and luck.

Are you kidding me? No kidding, the moment you realize and step aside from the idea that you'll ever get rich by winning the lottery, the moment you realize it's something you have to build, that's the moment you've stepped onto the path of humanity.

No man, no woman, can change the destiny the Gods have allotted us. We are born; our natal period is so effervescent. We grow through youth into adulthood, into humanhood. We grow into old age, we decline, and we terminate.

That is, as the Babylonians say, if the Gods don't call us *untimely* to our grave. There is an allotted equation. The sooner you realize it, the sooner you recognize and move on the fact that *you* need to prepare for the inevitable. You're a new creation, but that process cycles through the ages.

And in that respect, you *cannot* and *will not* be any different from any of the other individuals who have passed this way on Earth.

NOTES

Item / passage / page	Insight	Action

EVERY ADVERSITY BRINGS WITH IT THE SEED OF AN EQUIVALENT ADVANTAGE

Napoleon Hill wrote the words, and it was a statement that he frequently said: "Every adversity brings with it the seed of an equivalent advantage."

And this is a thing that we do need to keep in mind, because setbacks *do* come in the lives of all of us. The more we reach, the more chances we take, the more setbacks. And by the way, it's all the way up and down the board—whether it's love, war, or business, no matter your social status, we will always encounter setbacks.

So when we do, it's good to go back to the wisdom there to guide us—the wisdom that we can bounce back. Sometimes we can think, "Woe is me! They've cut back my income 15%!" or "I can't find another job!", and while that's not good, and that could be tough, and it could be true, there are ways that we can always wiggle around and make it work.

We're not refugees, by the way. We're not having our country attacked, and we're not fleeing with nothing but what we have in a bag at our side. We have opportunities and the chance to think about so much that we *do* have to do. It's a good time to call on our resources, one of those resources being our deeper drives and desires.

Are we dissatisfied because it's time for a change? Is that the universe telling us it's time for a change? Are we having these setbacks, multiples that seem to cluster around one particular train of action? Are we getting a cosmic message that it's time to consider going another way?

No, the new ways do not equal the old ways. But every adversity, every setback, every delay, brings with it the seed of an equivalent advantage.

NOTES

Item / passage / page	Insight	Action

INTERVENE AT THE LOWEST LEVEL OF RISK

You cannot live in this world without encountering conflict...so you would think that they would teach conflict resolution in schools. Of course, they don't. Not that there's no conflict there, but they certainly don't teach *effective* conflict resolution.

Let me give you one little idea which will serve you well in many, many ways, many, many different times. In conflict, or potential conflict, or touchy situations, always intervene at the lowest level you can.

In other words, I'm not saying you can't get mad. I'm not saying you can't throw your weight around, and I'm not saying you can't and shouldn't get an attorney on the case, if that's what it eventually requires. But I'm saying you're a fool if your first mention of anything is that you're going to sue.

Let's say you received an outrageous bill from the hospital. And of course, you know they've got this central intelligence bureau organized against you so that if you don't pay, it's going to go down on your credit record and make your life difficult.

They call it a social security number, but let's call it what it really is—a federally issued tracking number. They've got all this information organized using your social security number, and it's on file against you.

Millions of businesses and government busy-bodies access these data bases routinely. There is no privacy anymore, and the individual is subject to the state... The "system" has you in their grips.

So you're *mad—you're mad*! It's *unjust*! You're screaming, you're hollering.

First thing, calm down. Take a few deep breaths... Think of the last newborn infant you saw and touched... And, in your imagination, do it again, now... breath again.

Could it be that it is just a billing error? You wouldn't know until you did some preliminary work. It could just be that they're very willing to straighten it out because it was a billing error on their part, and they could apologize to you, too.

Going off the deep end is *always* counter-productive. Plus it's the nearest thing I know of to a sure-fire "you're going to end up with egg on your face" routine. And facial egg does not have any pleasing flavor associated with it, does it?

It's not necessary that you jump up, scream, swear, raise your blood pressure, and call your attorney first—catch my drift? And it could be, since we all know that people resist whenever something is pushed on them, that you can make things harder just because you are name-calling, belligerent, and loud.

Whereas, if you enter with a good will, but inquisitive, puzzled approach you could get everything resolved.

It's simpler, more effortless, and less stressful – totally dignified and elegant - to intervene at the lowest level of risk. That level of risk is always to say, "There's something here I don't understand. Can you help me with this?"

Later on, maybe, you will need to go see an attorney. But you certainly won't start there. You've got good sense. And certainly, you've heard it said that you can attract more flies with honey than you can with vinegar.

You should never act outside the bounds of dignity. There's no reason for you to – it's almost universally counter-productive.

Be bigger. Be tolerant. Work for understanding and embracement first. You'll be better off for it.

Be a human being, be proactive, be productive, do what you have to do.

HAVING A FAILURE OR A SETBACK ISN'T GOING TO AFFECT THE OUTCOME AT ALL

So many people give up when they meet their first defeat, when they get a setback, when they get a refusal, when they get a rejection, when they get a no. Obviously, we would say that's because they didn't have a firm enough designed desire to accomplish what it is they want to accomplish.

Being connected with LatinoLandia, I listen to a lot of my news in Spanish. I was listening to the news recently, and there was a story about a young gentleman, aged 17 or 18, who hit and killed a policeman.

He had done this trying to avoid a dragnet they had set up. I don't know what they were doing, and I don't know what *he* was doing. It could have been that he saw police stopping everybody. It could've been he was drinking. It could've been he was a criminal…that I don't know.

But the impression I got from the brief play on the radio was that the boy was trying to avoid the roadblock. And doing that, he lost control of his car and killed an officer, may he rest in peace. He died for his country… he died doing well.

And the boy—well, this is Mexico, so neither you nor I know what his fate will be. But the fate of the *normal* people that I talk to and work with on an everyday basis… a lot of them say they really want to achieve, a lot of them say they have tried but been defeated, and, of course, legions more never *really* tried, and were defeated. That was easy.

I'm talking about, what does it say? Well, let me ask you this—this was a failure for *la Ciudad de México,* for Mexico City, to lose a commissioned police officer. But do you *for one moment think* that they've ever even entertained the idea of not using these roadblocks, or stopping these dragnets, or whatever they call them? I know you know what I'm talking about.

Do you think they'd ever once talked about not using them anymore, and do you think the government of the United States has ever once decided maybe we shouldn't?

They could avoid seemingly needless deaths like this…

And how about the UK, how about Australia? How about Colombia? No, no, there are casualties, there are prices, there are errors, there are things that will go bad. That's the way it is. Those who know what they're doing prepare the best they can for those eventualities. And they suffer the price when they can't.

On a personal level, for the policeman's spouse and family, it's a tragedy. *God, bless his family!* For the city, the country, and the world, it's a statistic.

The police? They know what they're doing, and they know *why* they're doing it. And having a failure or a setback isn't going to affect their outcome at all. It isn't going to affect their practices at all.

Same way with you and me… We know exactly what we want, why, and we're engaged in getting it. Having a "failure" or a setback isn't going to affect the outcome at all.

TAKE CHARGE - CHANGE

When is the best time to start your new program, to open up to the new consciousness where you become a new person, where you adopt new habits, patterns, where you change your lifestyle to give you what you want?

When do *you* think now is the best time? This is a question that's come up throughout history. Paul of Tarsus said, "*Now* is the acceptable time!" That's what I think, too—now!

Especially when you think of the match-strike existence we live as humans. We have the ability to contribute, we have the ability to enjoy every day, we have the *ability*. We have the *potential*; as Bob Proctor says, "You were born *rich*—rich in potential to do anything you want, anything anyone else can do."

The question is, will you? The question is, will you let the programming you receive from the world at large, programming of limitation, lack, programming of war, conflict, programming of recession, depression, programming of "there's problems", programming of "money is tight"... Will you let *that* become your reality? Or are you going to take charge?

Know that it's an individual thing. You must be a value creator. In *any* economy, people are prospering. Now, taking charge might mean changing some of the things you've been doing that have kept you comfortable for so long. But, if you were comfortable being at the level you're at right now, you probably wouldn't even be reading these words, would you?

Yes, it's up to *you* to now change. And the answer to the question, "When?" is *"NOW!"*

NOTES

Item / passage / page	Insight	Action

WHO ELSE DO YOU KNOW WHO'S SUCCESSFULLY OUTRUN THE COPS?

People look at me and they see Ted Ciuba, America's foremost internet marketing consultant, circling the globe: Australia, New Zealand, Japan, Panamá, Dominican Republic, US and Canada; Singapore, Australia, Malaysia, China and points beyond. Seventy-seven different works, including *Mail Order in the Internet Age; How To Get Rich on the Internet,* Amazon.com bestseller; *The NEW Think and Grow Rich*, Amazon.com bestseller, dozens of books in The *Sub 4 Minute Extra Mile* Series. People hanging on my words, people paying me $50,000.00 to attend my private 2 day Destiny Creator Intensives.

But you know what? I know what the back seat of a squad car looks like from the inside out. Matter of fact, since the statute of limitations has expired, I can even share my crowning glory of those days. It was outrunning a string of lights and sirens one morning about 2 a.m. on my motorcycle. Boy, you talk about hot shit! Man, I've never had that thing perform like that! After about two and a half miles, though, I realized I wasn't going to continue to out-maneuver them. So I took an on-road motorcycle off-road.

Jumped a hill, slammed it down into horizontal position… That hot "tick, tick, tick, tick" of the overheated engine made me fearful it was going to catch fire. Floodlights were going over me just inches above my head… Yeah, they were searching for me. They were at all points. But they didn't catch me!

You see, I had a real rough youth. My mother had seven kids… Overwhelmed - six of them boys. Lived on the edge of a canyon. We could openly, and we did, defy her and do what we wanted. God bless her soul; I wish life had been different. Maybe I needed the experience to speak authentically. Who knows?

So, what turned it around, what stopped a life of jail and taking into a life of international fame, fortune, contribution, fulfillment? One book: *Think and Grow Rich* by Napoleon Hill.

Now it was a hard read, but I sensed it contained the secret. I meditated on it. I let it cure in me for years. Then I went back to it… I read it 77 times. And after spending several months with that book, several months later, my fortunes took off.

It's incredible what happened!

Fast forward. So, here I am circling the globe. I come back to these big cities like Singapore, London, Sydney, Atlanta every year, and I see some of the same people coming back that still haven't got it together. I decide I *must* teach them what turned it around for me, *Think and Grow Rich.*

And when I spoke it from the stage, when I interacted with people in coaching, it worked. When I gave them the book, everything was undone. It appeared to them - besides being antiquated - to be racist, sexist, nationalist. At one point I thought, "Hmm, I can re-write this public domain work."

And I instantly dove under the table, because that's like thinking you can re-write the Bible - and make it better. But then I realized there had been so many advances over the last 70 years… In aeronautics, in medicine, in media… Could personal achievement be any different?

In personal achievement there had been no quantum physics, there had been no Milton Erickson, there had been no neuro linguistic programming, there had even been no Tony Robbins. All of which changed the face of personal achievement dramatically!

That's what I bring to you in *The NEW Think and Grow Rich.* Yes, we added in woman, people of other nationalities and races - examples, quotes, stories from different times and cultures. That made it easier to read, and more a reflection of our times…

And for empowering the message of personal achievement? Now we have the quantum philosophy. We can speak in scientific language what Napoleon Hill would have had to have resorted to in mystic language, which could have killed his career in 1937, when the original was published.

Today *The NEW Think and Grow Rich* can empower you to achieve your dreams. To move up and live in a different house, to drive a different car, to send your kids to the schools that you want to send them to, to give them the advantages and the experiences that you want, to travel to your heart's content.

It's all available, no matter how bad your circumstances currently are.

One last point. Though today I live in a four-story luxury condo in Nashville, Tennessee and a high-rise condo in Panama City, Panama, at one point I was living in a $500 house. Not $500 a month; $500 total. A beat down single-axle camper trailer.

Now your situation could be worse than mine was. It's probably not as bad. I urge you to grab hold of this philosophy of empowerment, which is freely available to you, which can lift your spirits, correct your point of view, and give you wings to fly!

NOTES

Item / passage / page	Insight	Action

ONE MAN'S MOTHER'S DAY MUSINGS

"Mother, I know that Johnny Cash was one of your favorite artists, and I know that you liked his Christmas rendition of *The Little Drummer Boy*. And you liked it because the little boy at Christmas did what he could for the Christ. He didn't have money, he didn't have influence, but he could play a drum, and so he did.

"So Mother, in the same way, I offer you what I can do. I've lit a votive candle, which was a habit you had, that you taught me. As I write this article it's May 9, the evening before Mother's Day."

I've got an empty room with a hardwood floor downstairs. It's supposed to be the dining room. It's a new place, though—we haven't quite got everything in. And remember, we're living in two places, so there are different urgencies.

And on this little table is burning a candle—it's a vigil candle—and it's illuminating a portrait of my dear, deceased mother on the wall. My mother…when she had her power.

Generally we are so hep to the concept that *we* create our reality, that *we* can make anything happen. And while that's true, there are also very special moments that remind us, as I am reminded today, that there are things that we just have to live with and get on with.

My heart is hurting. I want to reach out to my mother, who according to her beliefs, is in Heaven.

And it should be an easy thing, but you know about the barrier between the world of the quick and the world of mystery peoples' spirits go to when they disappear from their bodies. And I'm thinking, "Wow, with all this empowerment, with all this truthfulness, because we see that people create their *own* destinies, there's still so much that is beyond our control at the same time."

Now, obviously I've lived with and gotten on with my mother being deceased. But on a day like this, when I don't have my mother and I'm burning a candle and I'm striving, what can I do? The best thing, the most significant thing I can do is to burn a candle and to write an article, so both of those I do.

But it's a poor replacement for the love that we receive from our mothers when they're alive.

So if your mother is alive, *cherish* her. Let her *know* that you love her. And of course, the ironic thing is that's not even necessary for a mother. No, because a mother's going to love you no matter what!

"Mother, I love you. Mother, I miss you. Mother, there's not a day and never will be a day that I'm not your son…"

Signed, Your little article boy.

"USE MY TIME! USE MY TIME! USE MY TIME!!"

The poet wrote, "There's a destiny that shapes our ends, rough hew them how we will." I've lost several friends and family members, some good friends in the internet community, and a father-in-law recently. Sad.

We all will die.

Then I happened to be looking through photo albums, family albums. Oh, all the people no longer here who formed important parts of my life! And that can be very, very sad, too.

"There is a destiny that shapes our ends, rough hew them how we will." And one of those things is we - like *all* of nature, whether we fill the allotted days of our species or go prematurely - are going to die.

We have an allotted time on Earth.

It's my suggestion, in addition to raising your kids and making a living, you decide to make a *contribution*. You know, many, many people have done it, and it's all because they made a *decision*.

I want to talk about one momentous event when I was visiting the Rosicrucian Egyptian Museum in San Jose, California USA… Oh, do I recommend it if you have any interest in Egyptian antiquities and you're in the United States! Obviously, if you're in Egypt, it's even better to be there.

At the park, near the administration building there's a colossal statute of Thutmose III, one of the patrons of literature, the arts, and writing, specifically. So, of course, he's a friend of mine.

So I am in this eternal HoloMagic moment… We're connected with the energies of ancient Egypt, who decided as a culture to make a difference. They made way more than just a living and survival. In fact those who did that, we don't even know where they are today, do we?

And the only wonder of the ancient world that still exists is the pyramids Egypt contributed.

It's 16 September 1987. I'm here with Thutmose and – while "praying" may not be the right word – I am in sync emotionally and spiritually. I am asking with an open heart, "How do I make my largest contribution? How do I do it? I know what I want to do."

I am out in front of the statute looking up, admiring, entering into it, talking, connecting. And then all of a sudden I am lifted into the air, a blinding light mystically burns behind me, ions change, and a powerful wind sweeps in… We become one, there's a mist that engulfs us, it connects us, surrounds us, infills me and it's like there's one mind, one spirit and one heart in ours.

Then the spirit assumes neuromuscular control, erects, and I'm seemingly shoved to the side in the presence of that high voltage energy, holding on to the inside of my body for dear life as that being mute 3,500 years speaks and words form through my vessel, my body. I hear Thutmose' voice in deep waves rolling through every dimension…

"Use my time! Use my time! Use my time!!"

Three times three. The triple trinity. It is done.

I believe these words were meant for you. Once you know what you want - and that takes time, effort, and connecting with your higher self - well here's a phrase consisting of 3 simple words repeated 3 times…That's the affirmation I received when Thutmose and I were sharing the same body, the same connection, the same energy space: "Use my time! Use my time! *Use* my time!"

It has helped me a lot because it reminds me of the briefness of life. Of the fact we can't escape death. Rough hew them how we will, there *is* a destiny that shape our ends; we will die. It has helped me make the right choice many, many times.

There's a magic significance that, should you choose to hear it, can charge your entire life.

And even if you believe in reincarnation, we're certainly going to die one lifetime at a time. You're not going to have the same identity, you're not going to be getting the same credit for being connected with what you did in a previous life, I don't care how kooky some people get about this, right?

"Use my time! Use my time! *Use* my time!" It reminds me of the imminence of death. It reminds me that… we don't know. My father-in-law died of what could ostensibly be called old age… It was over in seconds. Maybe age was contributing, I don't know.

But my buddy, younger than me, sporting accident, he went early. It flew from fun to fatal in a few seconds. We don't know what our allotted time is. We do know we can leave a legacy or we can leave just having skated by.

The choice is yours. If you are of the nature - and being with this philosophy I have a suspicion you might be - where you've decided how you want to contribute, you want to make a difference, and you want to leave a legacy, take this affirmation from Thutmose III straight from ancient Egypt…

"Use my time! U*se* my time! *Ussssee* my time!"

NOTES

Item / passage / page	Insight	Action

Index

"Now You Can Effortlessly Transmute Commuting Down-Time To Financial Independence!"

Announcing!

The NEW Think and Grow Rich In Audio

Rare Footage!

Word-for-word reading by the author, so you understand *every* word just as it was intended!

Not Available Anywhere Else!¡

Ted Ciuba expresses, emotes, renders, and interprets word-for-word the simple but deceptively complex information contained in the **13 named principles of *The NEW Think And Grow Rich* - *secrets*** <u>behind every millionaire's success</u> - none of which requires a thin dime.

Napoleon Hill First Discovered The Secret - Ted Ciuba Took It To New Heights In A New Age!

- Catch the true meaning and significance
- Tune into the emotions, vocal inflections, and all the other dimensions that give the *spoken* word superior communication ability over the written word!

The easiest way to fast-track your success!

Take *The NEW Think and Grow Rich*
At the "University on Wheels" - your car or transport!

www.TheNewThinkAndGrowRichAudio.com

It has a record setting history!

"Short, regular, focused, intense, intended training sessions could mean riches and fulfillment to *you!*"

Most intelligent people agree that to get ahead, you must go the extra mile. But the amazing thing is, it takes *so little* to excel!

After all, it's called the extra *mile*, not the extra *100 miles!*

Apart From Massive Intention, It Didn't Take Much

Roger Bannister
Runs sub 4 Minute Mile

Roger Bannister defied and redefined history by running the sub 4 minute mile. Exact time: 03:59.4/10's. 6 May 1954, Roger Bannister redefined human possibility by clocking in a mere 6/10's of a *second* sub 4 minutes.
And the amazing thing is that Bannister did NOT spend countless hours training... He gave it what he could in his busy pre-med schedule... A mere 30 minutes a day!!

And with that he set broke a barrier that had stood 3,000 years!

Then, within 2 1/2 years of Bannister's unachievable, record-breaking sub 4 minute mile, 18 others were doing it.

It's Your Turn! And now you can run the extra mile by tuning into a sub 4 minute length daily audio or video message with incredible motivation, insights, and training in a wide variety of fields always centered around the philosophy of *The NEW Think And Grow Rich.*

The compounding of simply sub 4 minutes every day is incredible!

You, too, can defy the status quo in **short, regular, focused, intense, intended training sessions** and **redefine what's possible for you!**

It takes so little to excel. Visit the website and get started today:

www.Sub4MinuteExtraMile.com

Additional Sub 4 Minute Extra Mile Volumes Available!

The entire line of training sessions in The *Sub 4 Minute Extra Mile* Series!

Entire Collection!
"Sub 4 Minute Extra Mile" Series
http://ThinkRich.com/sub4min

Full details on each title! Complete your collection! Give a meaningful gift!

Yours, *free!*

101 Success Secrets

From *The New Think And Grow Rich!*

Welcome!

101 Success Secrets
101 Training Sessions
101 Seconds Each

101SuccessSecretsFromTheNewThinkAndGrowRich.com

Celebrating the publication of *The New Think And Grow Rich* - **Revised Edition** - author Ted Ciuba put these video secrets together and makes them freely available to you. $197 value, *FREE!*

- 101 Success Secrets
- 101 Training Sessions
- 101 Seconds

Turn your life around. Stay focused. Achieve your dreams.

It's **all yours *free!***

"How Quickly Would Your Life Improve If You Began Using The Untapped 90% Of Your Brain To Bring You Wealth?!"

Revolutionary new neuroscience driven

Wealth Programming
Installs *The NEW Think and Grow Rich* Philosophy In You Effortlessly!

Amazing new neurosynergist® technology vaults leagues beyond ordinary hypnosis to effectuate immediate and permanent changes in your inner "wealth tracks"!

HoloMagic Wealth Programming

"Strap on your headphones, change your world!"

Wealth Programming is the *only* neural repatterning system in the world based on the proven principles of *The NEW Think And Grow Rich* using the patented neurosynergist® sound technology.

Dives to the depths of your *delta* subconscious, at the level where you connect with HoloCosm, and reprograms you to have and express the attitudes, strategies, and action-taking skills of the super wealthy.

Advanced thinkers, human potential experts, and the quantum and neuroscience labs affirm that the world you live in is a reflection of your inner world – the thoughts you consistently hold in your subconscious mind.

- Unleash the 90% realm of the brain that few people access and find your fortunes using the principles of *The NEW Think and Grow Rich!*...
- Put this cutting-edge, powerful, neural repatterning system to work for you!
- Visit:

www.HoloMagicWealthProgramming.com

Who Else Would Like To Have

The NEW Think and Grow Rich Author Ted Ciuba Motivate and Train Your Group?

Schedule permitting, Ted Ciuba welcomes keynote, speaking and training invitations from businesses, organizations, associations, and promoters.

The quantum performance message of *The New Think And Grow Rich* and *Sub 4 Minute Extra Mile* is perfectly suited to anyone in pursuit of money, a career, sales, and a life!

Through a brief but thorough pre-event questionnaire, Ted Ciuba makes each presentation unique to each group.

To discuss opportunities and arrangements contact our organization by email at events@holomagic.com or from the website at www.HoloMagic.com

Ted Ciuba On Stage In LA